M000014873

Kitchen Garden

A JOURNAL

by SUE PHILLIPS

Illustrated by ANNY EVASON

FRIEDMAN/FAIRFAX
PUBLISHERS

Contents

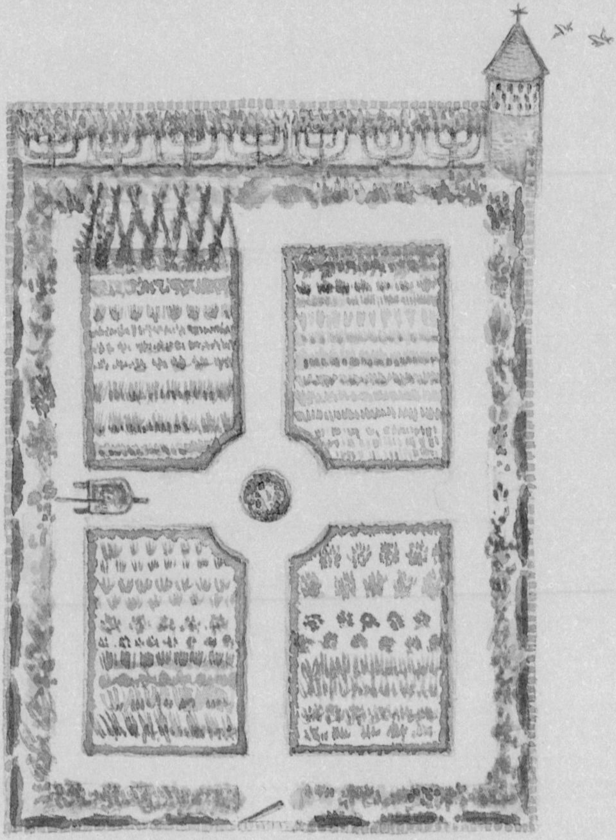

CHAPTER ONE

Kitchen Garden Styles

Introduction

*T*he first plant I ever grew was a giant summer squash (marrow), which my grandfather and I drip-fed with sugar-water through a string in its stem, and which had my name scratched on it when it was just 1in (2.5cm) long. By the end of the summer it was 3ft (1m) long, and too heavy to lift. I was just four at the time, but I've had a particular affection for edible gardening ever since. Wherever I've lived, I've grown something to eat. I think a small streak of self-sufficiency lies under the skin in most people, and there is nothing like starting in a small way to bring it out.

*W*hen I was a child, everyone we knew grew vegetables at the bottom of the garden. Ours was a neat patch occupying a quarter of the plot, where I remember pulling radishes and picking blackcurrants. The great attractions, from my point of view, were several huge fruit trees (ideal for climbing practice and tree-house camps), and the greasy, clay soil that made perfect pots when baked in the ashes of the bonfire. I'm sure it was this garden that set me on the road to a horticultural career. In later life, I again had a traditional kitchen garden, but then its charms were less obvious. It took up a huge amount of room, due to the generous spacings needed for access and to stop crops competing with one another for water and nutrients. For the amount of usable crops produced, it consumed a disproportionate amount of effort.

The Manor House Garden

*I*n Victorian times, grand country houses were not complete without their walled kitchen gardens. Ruled with a rod of iron by the head gardener–the outdoor equivalent of the butler–these provided fruit and vegetables for the kitchens and much more. Novelty crops, such as seakale and cardoons, which are rarely seen today, were Victorian favorites. Special greenhouses were equipped to force out-of-season luxuries, such as grapes, figs, and peaches, plus exotics, such as pineapples. The kitchen garden also provided all the cut flowers and potted plants used for floral decoration in the house, and it was the gardeners who did the arrangements. The Victorian kitchen garden was, first and foremost, a status symbol. House guests would be escorted around the garden by their host so they could admire the magnificence of his domain. The traditional layout included a central path, flanked by extravagant flower borders, down which visitors promenaded, and which provided a decorative foreground to all the neat rows of vegetables and the scurrying staff beyond.

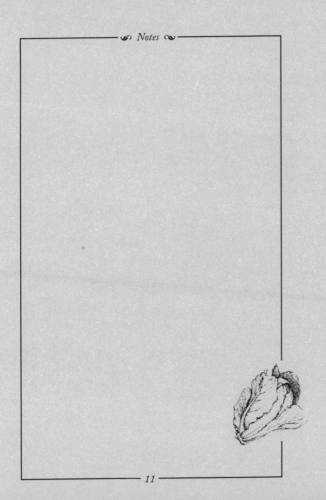

Potagers

*P*otagers are fashionable and decorative alternatives to traditional kitchen gardens. The name comes from the grand, formal vegetable gardens of France, such as that at the Chateau Villandry, where a series of geometrically shaped beds, edged with boxwood, provide produce for the house. Potagers are easy to adapt to a more modest scale and, because they are so decorative, they are ideal for small gardens where crops cannot be hidden from view. A modern potager could incorporate flowers for cutting, a seat, deep or raised beds, and walls or trellises to support climbers, such as vines. Instead of boxwood, beds may be edged with tiles, clipped evergreen herbs, or rows of flowers, in keeping with the style of the rest of the garden.

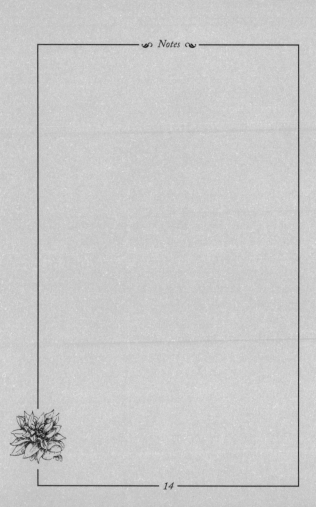

Deep Beds

Having discovered the benefits of deep beds, I wouldn't consider growing vegetables in any other way. Cultivating the soil very deeply and adding lots of well-rotted compost or manure allows roots to travel downward instead of sideways for their water and nutrients. This means you can grow plants much closer together than you would in a conventional garden. You can reduce spacings by one third, and can dispense altogether with paths between the rows, so you grow much more in the same space. Deep beds are less work too. Because the plants are grown close together, they soon fill the rows and smother out weeds, so less hoeing is needed. Plants grow better too, since the soil is never walked on, and stays uncompacted. All the work is done from the paths around the beds.

The Ornamental Kitchen Garden

I'm a passionate cottage gardener, *and* have long been fascinated by the idea of flowers and vegetables growing together in glorious disarray in my borders. Sadly, in reality, vegetables grown among flowers merely attract record numbers of slugs, and fail to make proper hearts, or reach full size, due to competition and shading from their floral neighbors. It is possible to compromise, by planting colorful varieties of popular vegetables, which are just as tasty as the green ones, in a decorative bed, or by growing a suitable flowers among complementary–and widely spaced–vegetables.

Patios and Balconies

*I*n gardens too tiny for a conventional kitchen garden, cultivate a pretty, potted version in containers. Choose a sunny, sheltered corner of the patio, and grow decorative crops, such as zucchini, sweet peppers, and eggplants (aubergines). Grow pole beans, sugar snap peas (mangetout), cucumbers, and outdoor tomatoes in tubs, and support their stems with ornamental pagodas or spires of bunched willow wands. Use tubs at the bases of pergola poles or trellises to grow kiwis or grape vines. Half-barrels are large enough to grow dwarf fruit trees—orange and lemon trees will thrive outdoors in summer, even in cooler regions. Save hanging baskets for tiny, trailing tomatoes or a mixture of herbs.

ᴥᴥ

*T*he secret of success with potted kitchen gardens is water. As a general rule, the smaller the container, and the more plants it holds, the more often it will need watering—up to twice daily in hot summers. Regular feeding is vital if your potted kitchen garden is to produce tasty, tender crops. Use liquid tomato fertilizer or an organic equivalent containing a good range of trace elements, which are essential for flavor, plus a liquid seaweed extract.

*I*ndoor Gardens

*I*n cooler regions, you can grow exotic fruits in a conservatory. Opt for standard-trained citrus trees and potted figs, with passionfruit climbing up the walls and along the rafters and miniature bananas trees and guavas in tubs. Try olive trees, which naturally make craggy shapes reminiscent of Mediterranean groves or grow grape vines trained as standards—all gnarled trunks and leafy heads dripping with fruits.

*Y*ou can even have a vegetable garden indoors. I raise salad sprouts in jars, rinsing the seeds twice daily with clean water through cheesecloth (muslin) lids. Most varieties are ready to eat within a few days. Alfalfa (lucerne), tasting of fresh garden peas, is my favorite, and is also the fastest to grow. Setting the jars on a windowsill helps the sprouts to green up, which gives them the best flavor. Mung beans (Chinese bean sprouts) produce the largest crop, but I usually add a few fenugreek seeds for their tangy taste.

A kitchen windowsill makes a good winter herb garden. Pot up a few roots of mint, dug up from the garden. They should start sprouting in a few weeks. I raise herbs, such as flat-leaved parsley, chervil, and basil, in pots. There is no need to thin out the seedlings or transplant to larger pots—start snipping as soon as they are big enough, then sow new pots when the old ones are half used.

Heirloom Vegetables

Some gardeners specialize in growing heirloom vegetables—old varieties that are rarely found in seed catalogs. These have been saved from extinction by enthusiasts because the vegetables have special attributes, such as taste or appearance, that make them worth preserving. Today, a few seed suppliers specialize in heritage vegetables, and there are seed exchange programs that you can join.

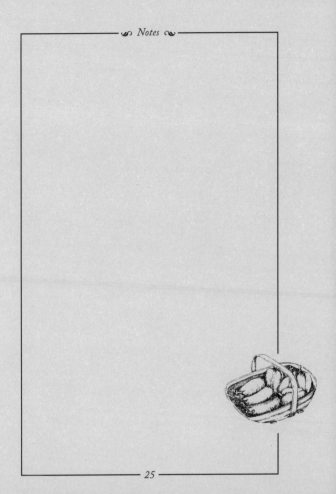

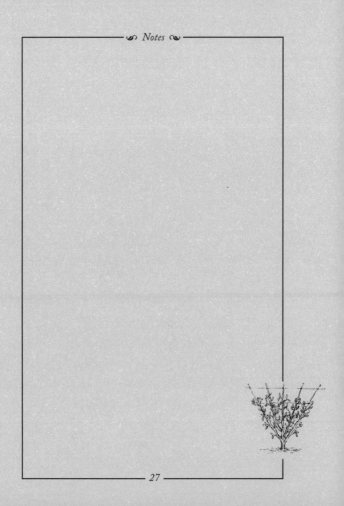

CHAPTER TWO

Growing Know-How
Vegetables

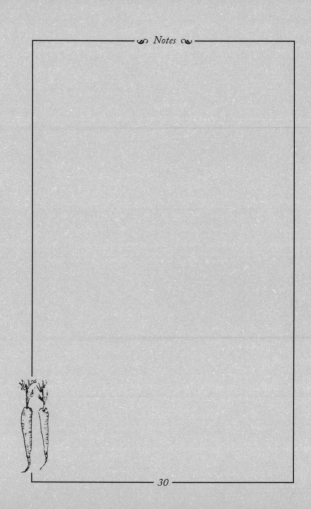

To grow healthy, succulent, tender vegetables, a good site is essential so the crops can grow quickly. Vegetables need plenty of light; the kitchen garden should be in sun for most of the day. (In light shade, only leafy crops, such as cabbages or lettuces, will do well.) Shelter is important too–strong winds can damage crops, or blow them over. The soil should be deep, rich, and fertile, full of organic matter to help retain moisture, and completely free of perennial weeds. Tough, stringy, or tasteless vegetables or early bolting are signs that the growing conditions are not right–rectify them, and all will be well.

Brassicas

Brassicas, which include Brussels sprouts, cabbages, cauliflowers, and broccoli, must have firm soil–without it, they do not form proper hearts. With the exception of spring cabbages, which are sown in midsummer, brassicas should be sown in midspring. You can buy container-grown plants, but you run the risk of importing root diseases into your garden on their roots, so grow your own from seed, if possible. Sow in an outdoor seedbed and transplant the seedlings to their final positions when they are a few inches (centimetres) high. For early crops in cooler regions, raise young plants in a greenhouse and plant out when the soil has warmed up. Spacings vary, depending on which brassicas you grow, but as a rough guide, plants should be spaced the same distances apart as their ultimate heights. Cauliflowers are notorious for running to seed in dry soil, so water them regularly. You can speed up growth by watering the plants with a liquid fertilizer.

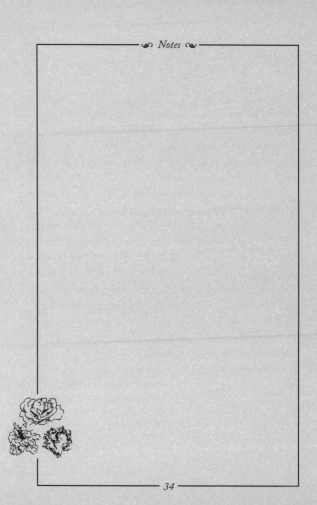

— ❧ *Notes* ❧ —

Leafy Vegetables

Oriental greens, spinach, and Swiss chard are all fast-growing, leafy crops that need the same conditions as lettuces. High temperatures and dry soil can cause plants to bolt. Sow spinach and Swiss chard in mid- to late spring; thin the seedlings to leave spinach 3in (7.5cm) apart and Swiss chard 12in (30cm) apart. Start picking outside leaves as soon as they are big enough to use, leaving the rest of the plant to grow on. Spinach will bolt rapidly as the temperature rises, and must be re-sown regularly, but one sowing of Swiss chard should last all season. (In potagers, containers, or ornamental kitchen gardens, grow the red-stemmed variety known as rhubarb, or ruby chard, which tastes just as good, but looks more decorative.) Oriental greens need warm weather if they are to grow well–low temperatures will cause them to bolt early–so don't sow them until midsummer. Harvest whole plants as soon as they are large enough, and when they have formed tight hearts. Cook them in stir-fries.

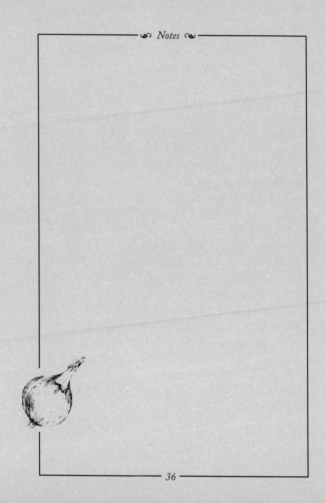

Notes

Bulbs and Stems

The easiest way to grow onions is by planting "sets," which resemble small bulbs, in early spring. Press each set, blunt-end down, into the soil, and give a half turn to "screw" it in place. Unless the base comes into contact with the soil, the set will not root. Plant garlic the same way, using the largest cloves separated from a large head, or buy cloves from a seed supplier. Leeks belong to the same family as onions. Grow them from seeds sown in spring in an outdoor seedbed. Thin them out to 1in (2.5cm) or more apart, then transplant the seedlings when they are large enough to handle. Grow leeks 4in (10cm) apart each way in deep beds for tall white stems, or 12in (30cm) apart in rows 6in (15cm)

apart in conventional plots for larger plants. Leeks are ready to eat in autumn and winter. If a few plants run to seed, you can include the fluffy seedheads in dried flower arrangements.

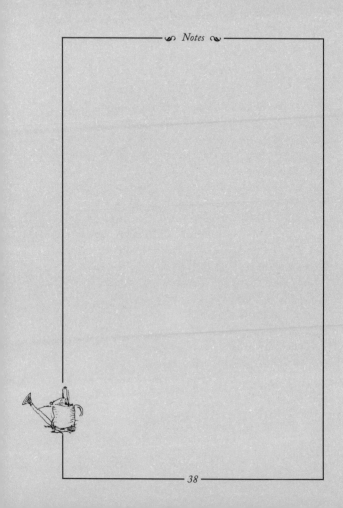

Notes

Celery

Celery is regarded, even by seasoned vegetable growers, as a challenge. Plants are notoriously fickle and will run to seed at the first opportunity. The right soil is essential. It must be deep, rich, and well manured–really packed with organic matter. To raise plants, sow seeds in flats (seed trays) of potting mix in a heated propagator at 60°F (15°C) in midspring, and transplant the seedlings into individual pots when they are large enough to handle. Temperature is crucial at this stage. If it drops below 50°F (10°C) there is a good chance plants will bolt later, however good their growing conditions. If you don't have the facilities to grow from seed, buy pot-grown plants and plant them out after the last frosts. Space them 12in (30cm) apart in rows 15in (40cm) apart, water well and feed regularly with nitrogen-rich liquid fertilizer–it is vital that the plants' growth is not checked, as they will bolt or become tough and stringy. Dig them up in late summer or fall, when they are large enough to use.

Asparagus

Asparagus plants are perennial, so instead of growing them in the vegetable garden, prepare a separate bed for them. Dig deeply, burying large quantities of rich organic matter. Seaweed is especially beneficial (asparagus does not mind small amounts of salt), or use seaweed meal from an organic gardening supplier. If the ground is well drained, asparagus will grow in a level bed. On wet or clay soil, construct a raised bed 6in (15cm) or more above ground level or plant on top of ridges in the traditional way. Asparagus plants are sold in early spring as dormant crowns–spread the roots out well and plant in a shallow trench, covering them with 2in (5cm) of soil. As the season progresses, gradually hill up the plants until the trench is filled. Nurseries and garden centers sometimes sell pot-grown plants, and these are best planted in early summer. Choose all-male varieties, as these have thick, succulent stems. Feed and mulch asparagus beds heavily every spring. Don't cut any spears the year after planting. Take a few the next year, and slowly increase after that. Always allow the foliage to die down naturally in fall–don't cut it back early.

Notes

Globe Artichokes

*G*lobe artichokes are also perennials. If space is short, grow them in flower borders. Otherwise, make a separate bed for them in the kitchen garden. The plants resemble decorative thistles, with soft, spiky, silver-green foliage from which 4-5ft- (12-15m-) tall flower stems appear in summer. The edible part is the flower bud, which should be picked when tightly shut and about the size of a fist. Plant offsets or pot-grown plants in spring, 3ft (1m) apart each way, and water well. You can expect one or two heads the first year, but plants come into full cropping the second year. Cut suitable buds as they appear, with a few inches (centimetres) of stem. In fall, cut down the stems and protect the crowns with straw. After four years, crowns are past their best–dig them up in early spring, separate the young offsets from the edge of the clump, and replant them in a new spot.

Fruiting Vegetables

*A*mong the many varieties of tomatoes available today are some that remain green when they are ripe and others that ripen to a creamy or pale yellow color, described as "white" in seed catalogs. You will also find striped tomatoes, yellow tomatoes, tiny, bite-sized cherry tomatoes, and giant, beefsteak tomatoes. Large tomatoes take longer to ripen than standard varieties, and cherry tomatoes need less water. Taste several varieties to find which you prefer before you decide what to grow. Tomatoes need rich soil with lots of humus and plenty of warmth and sunlight. (A greenhouse gives a longer picking season in cool climates.) Space the plants 2ft (60cm) apart and support them with stakes. Remove sideshoots from all but determinate (bush) varieties to encourage heavier cropping. Feed regularly with a high-potash liquid tomato fertilizer, or an organic one, such as comfrey liquid and leave the fruits on the vines until they have ripened completely and developed their full flavor.

Peppers and Eggplants

*P*eppers and eggplants are short, bushy plants that produce prolific crops continuously from mid- to late summer. They need the same care as tomatoes, but prefer a warmer temperature—a greenhouse is essential in all but the warmest climates. A well-sheltered south-facing patio or a greenhouse are ideal There is no need to remove sideshoots, but each plant should be tied to a short stake for support. The stems of pepper plants are brittle and snap easily, and eggplant stems are very prickly, which makes it difficult to harvest the fruits. You can pick eggplants and green peppers as soon as they are big enough to use, but if you want red peppers, leave green ones on the plant to ripen—this takes about six weeks, and the plants will not set more fruits while they are ripening.

Peas

*P*eas look great growing in my garden, but picking and podding them seems to take forever—and what I get in the pan sometimes makes me wonder if it was all worthwhile. If that is how you feel, then grow sugar snap peas, whose pods are eaten whole, thus dispensing with the time-consuming task of shelling. Either sow seeds in situ, 1in (2.5cm) deep, or—especially where rodents or soil pests are a problem—sow indoors in flats and plant out when the seedlings are a few inches (centimetres) high. Grow peas in neutral to alkaline soil, 3in (7.5cm) apart in triple rows with a 3ft- (1m) wide path between them and the neighboring crop. Push 4ft- (1.2m) long twiggy sticks into the ground beside the plants so they can support themselves with their tendrils. When flowers appear, spray against pea moth (*Cydia migricana*), and when the first pods are visible, cover the plants with netting to protect them from birds. Pick the pods while they are still young, tender, and tasty— don't wait for them to grow large and fat—they will not taste so good.

Beans

*B*eans come in an incredible number of varieties. Some grow only 1ft (30cm) high, need no support, and quickly produce a tasty crop. Pole beans take longer to start cropping because they need to grow up poles or netting first, but they produce beans over a longer period. Some beans are best eaten fresh, while others can be dried and stored for cooking in winter soups and stews (this group incudes some of the best heritage varieties.) As a general rule, sow seeds 1in (2.5cm) deep, or set out young, pot-grown plants when all danger of frost is past. If beans fail to "set," suspect cold weather, birds pecking off the flower buds, or dry conditions–spray the flowers with water every day in dry weather and soak the roots well.

Sweet Corn

Sweet corn needs a large area in which to grow, but it is worth every inch of the space which it occupies. The taste of shop-bought cobs can't compare with the flavor of those picked from the garden and put straight into the cooking pot. As soon as the cobs have been picked, their sugars begin to turn to starch and the flavor is quickly impaired. Sow seeds ½in (1.5cm) deep in late spring. (In cold regions, sow in pots under glass and plant out in early summer, after the last frosts.) Corn plants are pollinated by wind, so sow or plant in large, square blocks instead of rows, and space the plants 18in (45cm) apart each way. That way, each plant has several neighbors to ensure good pollination–expect about two cobs per plant. Water well in dry weather, and tap the flower tassels to help pollination. The cobs are ready when the kernels are creamy gold in color and squirt milky juice when pressed with a fingernail–peel back part of the green husk to test them. Pick and cook them right away.

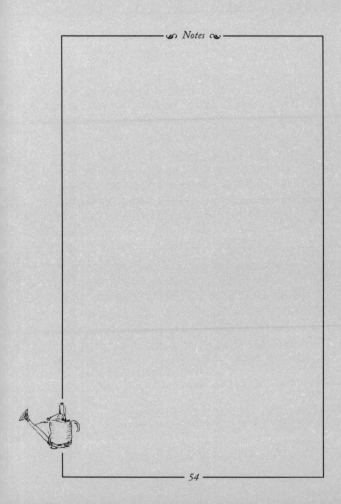

Roots

Home-grown root vegetables are delicious, particularly when they are grow organically. Carrots do
not have the usual "soapy" taint and beets taste sweet
and juicy. Besides the well-known kinds, try more
unusual roots, such as salsify, which is a real gourmet
treat. Root vegetables need the right conditions if they
are to grow well. If the soil contains too much
nitrogen, they will fork and be difficult to peel. Stony
soil causes them to bend and twist to avoid the
obstructions. Deep, light soil is best, and it should have
been well manured before the previous crop was grown.
Root crops don't transplant well, so it's best to sow
them in situ. Space the rows 12in (30cm) apart. When
the seedlings emerge, thin them out, first to 1in
(2.5cm) apart, then later to 3in (7.5cm) for carrots, and
6in (15cm) for salsify. Sow seeds in the same year that
you buy them, because they do not remain viable for
long. Never allow the soil to dry out while the seeds are
germinating.

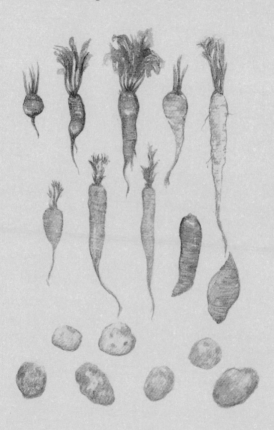

Potatoes

Some gardeners believe it isn't worth growing their own potatoes because they are so cheap to buy, but there is one good reason to do so—flavor. Choose varieties bred for taste rather than yield, and opt for early varieties; their flavor, when lifted straight from the garden and cooked with mint and butter, is second to none. Potatoes are very easy to grow. Plant tubers 5in (12.5cm) deep. Space early varieties 12in (30cm) apart in rows 24in (60cm) apart, and maincrop varieties 15in (45cm) apart in rows 30in (75cm) apart. In deep beds, plant early varieties 15in (45cm) apart each way and maincrops 24in (60cm) apart each way. As the stems appear, gently hill them up by drawing soil around them with a rake. Do this several times in early summer, until the foliage meets between the rows. Lift new potatoes when the first tubers are big enough to use (feel around in the soil to find out). Lift only as many as you need, and leave the rest to grow on. Leave second-early potatoes in the ground until the plants begin to flower, then lift them as you need them. Maincrop potatoes should be left in the ground until the end of the season, then lifted and stored for winter.

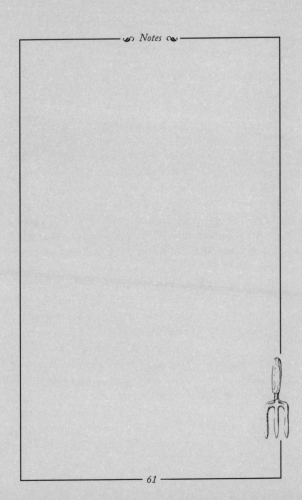

Salad Crops

Lettuces are the best-known salad
crop. There are regular hearting
kinds, crisp-hearted varieties, and
upright romaine (cos) lettuces. Red
or green frilly types and oak-leaved
varieties do not form hearts—just cut a
loose head of leaves when the plants are large enough.
With "cut-and-come-again" lettuces, you can pick
leaves as you need them, and leave the rest on the plant
to grow on. Apart from the "cut-and-come-again"
varieties, sow lettuce seeds little and often for a
continuous supply. They need light if they are to
germinate, so cover them only lightly
with soil, but keep them well
watered, or they won't grow.
Thin out the seedlings (don't
try to transplant them in
warm weather) to 12in
(30cm) apart. Water the
plants well in dry weather
and feed with a nitrogen-
rich liquid fertilizer.

Salad greens are the fastest
growers in the vegetable plot.
These include arugula
(rocket), lamb's lettuce
(corn salad), sorrel, and
purslane. Other leafy
crops, such as chicory,
endive, and spinach, can be
harvested young, as baby
leaves. For really creative salads,
grow several types at the same time or thinly sow a
mixture of any of these, plus lettuce seeds, and snip the
seedlings when they are a few inches
(centimetres) high. (This mixture

can also be grown on a sunny
windowsill indoors in
winter.) Grow salad greens
in the same way as lettuces;
they don't form hearts, and
can be grown 1-2in (2.5-5cm)
apart. To ensure a constant
supply, sow little and often—
about every two weeks.

Squash

Squashes are good vegetables to interest children in gardening. The plants grow so quickly you can almost see the fruits swell. Depending on variety, they have bright red, bluish, or gold rinds, often decorated with blotches, speckles, or stripes. Sow the seeds in late spring after the last frosts, in rich soil, or on top of the compost heap. Feed the plants regularly with liquid tomato fertilizer and watch them take off. Pick summer squashes, including zucchini, when they are large enough to eat—the more you pick, the more you will get. Leave winter squashes on the vine to ripen in fall, but bring them under cover before the first frosts. Store them in a cool room or a frost-free shed or garage until you need them.

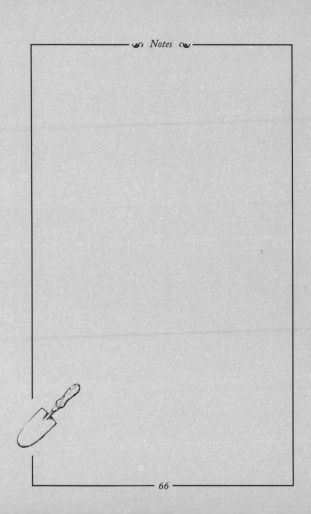

Cucumbers

Nowadays, even if you don't have a greenhouse, it is possible to grow good cucumbers in cooler regions if you choose modern outdoor varieties—they are as good as the indoor kind. To raise your own plants, sow seeds in a heated propagator at 70-80°F (21-27°C). Gradually lower the heat after the seedlings appear, to accustom them to colder conditions before planting them out. Alternatively, you can buy plants and set them out in the garden. Plant indoor cucumbers in an unheated greenhouse in late spring and outdoor varieties in the open in early summer, well after the last frosts. Plant on a small mound of soil and always water around the base of the mound to avoid neck rot, which can kill young plants. Water sparingly at first, but increase both watering and liquid feeding (use tomato fertilizer) as growth speeds up. Tie stems to stakes for support. All-female varieties are easier to grow and more productive. Cucumbers grow straight from the main stem of the plant. Remove sideshoots and tendrils but take care not to break off flowers—baby cucumbers develop behind these when the petals are over. Cut cucumbers as soon as they fill out their shape.

Melons

Melon plants are almost identical to those of cucumbers, and are cultivated in exactly the same way. Cantaloupes are best suited to outdoor temperatures, as they ripen quickly. In cold regions, plants produce more fruits if they are grown in a cold frame or greenhouse. Train the plants up canes in a greenhouse, and let them run over the ground in a cold frame. In the open, let them run over the ground or put up a low netting "fence" for them to climb over, to keep the fruits clear of the soil. The flowers need to be pollinated in order to set fruit. Outdoors, if there are plenty of bees around, they will do the job, but you will need to hand-pollinate plants under glass. Pick off a fully open male flower, remove the petals, and dab the flower into the center of a female flower. (They have an embryo melon behind the petals.) Leave the melons on the vine until they are completely ripe and have a musky scent. Test for ripeness by gently pressing the tip of the fruit around the old flower scar, with your thumbs. If it yields slightly, the melon is ready to eat.

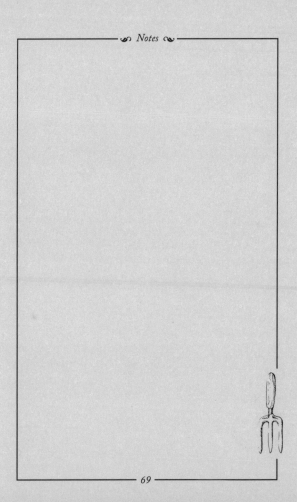

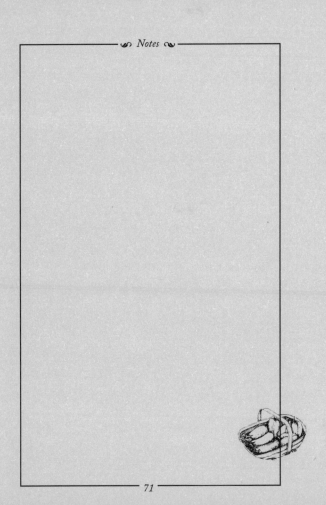

∽ Notes ∾

Mushrooms

*V*ictorian gardeners grew mushrooms in pretty containers and brought them indoors for table decorations. The traditional way of growing them was very hit-or-miss, involving mushroom spawn on the lawn or piles of fermenting manure whose temperature had to be taken regularly. Nowadays, mushroom growing is simplicity itself. You can buy a kit containing ready-spawned blocks of compost, which comes complete with growing instructions. Kept in the dark, at room temperature, a good crop of mushrooms should appear within a few weeks. With luck, the value of the crop will almost equal the price of the kit. All kinds of mushrooms, including the more exotic types, such as shiitake, are available in kits, and make fascinating growing.

Herbs

The most popular culinary herbs are basil, chives, French tarragon, marjoram, mint, parsley, rosemary, sage, and thyme; all have robust flavors, and, with the exception of French tarragon, are hardy plants that can live outdoors all year round, even in cooler regions. (Parsley is a biennial, but new plants should be grown every spring.) As a useful "second string" you could include herbs such as chervil, and summer savory. Chervil and summer savory are hardy, but basil can't be

put outdoors until after the last frost. Herbs with an oriental flavor are fashionable now, too; try cinnamon or lemon basil, coriander, and lemon grass. Plant herbs in geometric patterns in formal herb gardens, use them to edge a potager, or plant a mixture in a row in a kitchen garden. To stop invasive kinds, such as mint and horseradish, from spreading, grow them in large pots sunk up to their rims in the garden. Most herbs grow well in containers; grow a group in a large planter, or hanging basket.

Edible Flowers

Edible flowers make pretty additions to salads and are good garnishes and table decorations. Suitable kinds to use whole include borage, English violets, nasturtiums, and primroses. Separate the florets of lavender flowers, and pull the petals from pot marigolds, daisies, and chive flowers. All of these can be picked from the garden or grown for extra decoration among salad crops anywhere where they will not be swamped by vegetation. Edible flowers can be frozen in cubes of ice, or candied (crystallized) to make cake decorations.

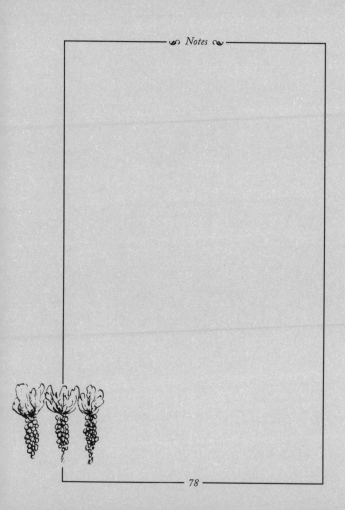

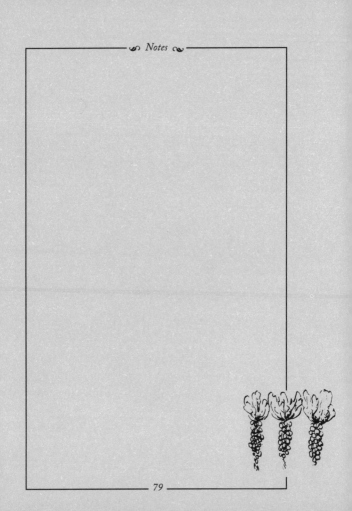

CHAPTER THREE

Growing Know-How Fruit

~⚬~

*F*ruit trees and bushes need a sunny, sheltered site, facing away from the early-morning sun. Otherwise, in spring, when the trees are in blossom, early sun can scorch frosted petals. If this happens, the flowers will not be visited by pollinating insects and the trees will not produce fruits. The soil should be deep, fertile, and well drained. Before planting, dig deeply, mixing in plenty of well-rotted garden compost, manure, or other organic matter, and some general fertilizer. If you want to train fruit trees against a wall, put up trellises, or wall nails and wires to support them before planting. Cane fruits, such as blackberries and loganberries, need posts and horizontal wires to support them. Every spring, sprinkle some general fertilizer around the plants, and mulch the ground thickly. A high-potash feed in late summer is also beneficial.

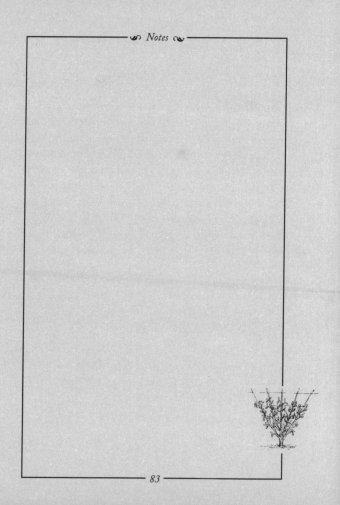

Apples and Pears

*A*pples and pears are the easiest tree fruits to grow. A young tree bought from a nursery will have been trained into shape. Choose one grown on a dwarfing rootstock, if you want it to remain compact and to start fruiting within a few years. Unless there are plenty of fruit trees growing in your area, you will need to grow two different varieties that are capable of cross-pollinating to be sure of getting fruit. Ask your nursery or garden center to suggest compatible varieties. If you want to plant your fruit trees in grass, leave a circle of

bare earth 3ft (1m) in diameter around the bases of the trunks so that the young trees don't have to compete with the grass for water and nutrients. In winter, when the trees have lost their leaves, prune to thin out crowded shoots and to keep the center of the tree open. The branches should form a goblet shape. Cut out dead, diseased, and damaged shoots whenever they appear. If space is very short, choose a family tree, which has several different varieties grafted onto one trunk. Both dessert and cooking apples can be produced on the same tree, and they will all pollinate one another.

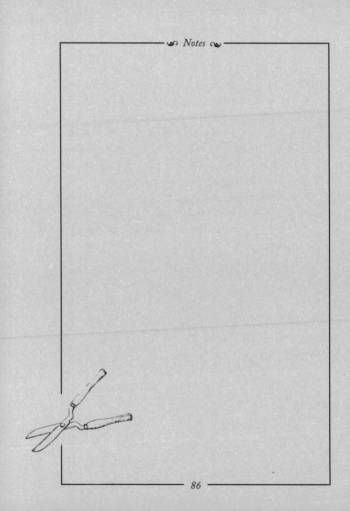

Cherries and Plums

*T*he dwarfing rootstocks available for cherry and plum trees have less effect on the ultimate size of the trees than do those for apples and pears, so be prepared for these trees to grow to a height of at least 15ft (4.5m), and almost as much across. Expect them to take five years before they begin to produce reasonable crops. Buy well-shaped trees with several strong branches evenly spaced around their trunks. Most cherries and plums need cross-pollinating, but some are self-fertile. If you have room for only one tree in your garden, ask at your nursery or garden center for advice on the best variety to choose. Plant the tree, allowing plenty of room for it to grow. Tie it to a stake for support and leave bare earth around the base of the trunk for the first five years—after that, you can allow grass to grow up to the trunk and underplant with spring bulbs if you like. If you bought a well-shaped tree, the only pruning you will need to do will be to cut out any dead, diseased, or dying shoots when you see them. When the fruits are still green, drape the trees with netting to protect them from birds, and leave them to ripen fully before you pick them.

Figs

*F*ig trees are naturally heat- and drought-tolerant once they are established, and are ideal for many "problem" situations. They can be grown as bushes or trees, trained as fans against a wall (a good way of providing extra warmth and shelter for them in cooler regions), or grown in pots on the patio. Left unrestrained, a fig tree can grow huge. To keep it compact and to increase its fruiting potential, you will need to confine its roots. Dig a hole 3ft (1m) square, line it with old bricks and rubble, then fill it with a mixture of good topsoil mixed with well-rotted compost, and plant into that. In cold regions, when the leaves fall, remove any partly grown figs, as they will not live through the winter and may become infected. Prune the tree in late winter, when it is completely dormant—if you prune during the growing season it will bleed badly and the sap loss may seriously weaken it. Leave the figs on the tree until the skins change color and the fruits feel slightly soft when squeezed.

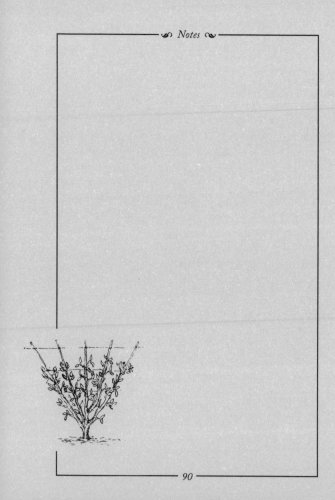

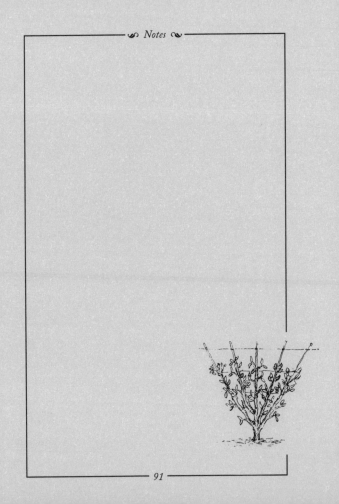

Containerized Fruit Trees

Dwarf fruit trees in pots make good plants for a patio. Choose naturally compact trees. Patio peaches are perfect; these are genetic dwarfs with pretty blossoms and full-sized fruits. Apple trees that have been trained as bushes on very dwarfing rootstocks, small standard trees, or upright cordons are also good. With the exception of fig trees, most other fruit trees are too vigorous to be happy in containers for long. Containerized figs can be grown as either bushes or standard trees, but they must be fed and watered copiously in summer to prevent fruit drop. Containers for fruit trees should be at least 18in (45cm) in diameter. Fill them with good, soil-based potting mix, water copiously in spring and summer, and feed weekly with a liquid tomato fertilizer–potted trees shed their fruits if their roots are deprived of moisture. In fall and winter, water only when the growing medium looks dry and protect plants from wind and excess wet. In severe weather, the roots of containerized trees may freeze in their pots–protect them by wrapping the containers in bubble plastic or plunge them up to their rims in a garden bed.

Raspberries

Raspberries like lime-free soil–in alkaline soil they suffer from mineral deficiencies, but you can counteract these, to a certain extent, by feeding the bushes with sequestered iron in spring and summer. Summer-fruiting raspberries grow vigorously, and need lots of space. Prune them as soon as all the fruits have been picked. Cut all the stems that carried fruit to ground level, but leave the new shoots, which will carry next year's crop. Thin out excess canes, leaving the best spaced 9in (23cm) apart. Tie these to post-and-wire fencing for support. If time and space are short, grow fall-fruiting varieties instead. These ripen in late summer and fall, when fresh raspberries are scarce in the shops. You can grow them in a bed, which means you get more fruit from less space. Birds are less likely to take the fruits but, in cold regions, the crop may be cut short by early frosts. Prune in early spring by cutting all the canes down to ground level. The new shoots that grow in the summer will carry the next season's crop.

Strawberries

*Y*ou can grow strawberries spaced 1ft (30cm) apart each way in conventional beds or in tubs, hanging baskets, or strawberry planters. Buy young plants in fall or spring, plant them right away, and keep them well watered. If you are growing them in beds, spread clean straw around the plants or use strawberry mats, to keep the fruits clean and prevent mold. As the fruits swell, cover the plants with netting to protect them from birds. Raise the netting slightly above the plants on a

framework of canes to prevent the birds from pecking
through it, but make sure it
is tucked well in around the
plants, to stop birds from
becoming trapped underneath it.

Pick ripe fruits daily, and when
the whole crop has been harvested clip over
the plants to remove old fruit stems and foliage,
then sprinkle a high-potash fertilizer between them
and water it in. Keep containerized strawberries well
watered, and feed them weekly with high-potash liquid
tomato fertilizer. If you want early fruits, move the
pots to the greenhouse in early spring.

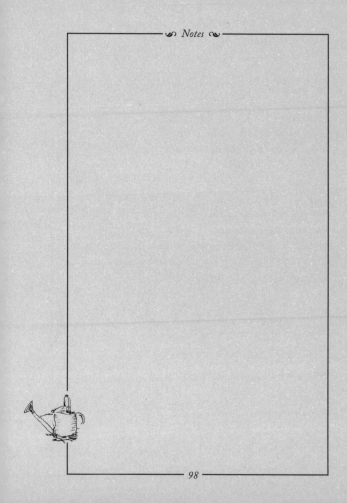

Blueberries

*I*n very acid soil, the only fruit that grows well is blueberries. The bushes produce clusters of bell-like, white flowers in summer, followed by blue-black fruits with a powdery "bloom." In fall the foliage takes on fiery tints, and the plants are decorative enough to grow as ornamental shrubs. Yields are improved if two plants of different varieties are grown to cross-pollinate each other, but many varieties will set fruit even when grown alone. Blueberries need plenty of water during the growing season. If your garden soil is not suitable, you can grow them in pots. Use an ericaceous potting mix, and feed weekly with liquid tomato fertilizer from early to late summer. The fruits are ready to pick as soon as they turn blue-black. Birds love them, so protect the plants with netting. Grow other heathland fruits, such as cranberries, in the same way.

Gooseberries

Gooseberries grow on dense spiny bushes, which makes it difficult to pick the fruits. If you prune the plants so that the branches are well spaced, you'll get larger fruits, and they will be easier to pick. Prune in winter when the bushes are leafless; thin out congested branches and cut back new growth by half. Alternatively, grow them as cordons, and prune them in summer, cutting back all sideshoots to just beyone the point where the fruits are growing. Feed and mulch the bushes in spring, and keep them well watered when the fruits are swelling. You can pick gooseberries for cooking before they are fully developed, or use the trimmings from a large crop for fruit tarts. Leave dessert varieties on the bushes until they ripen in midsummer. The fruits are ready to eat when they have changed color and feel slightly soft when squeezed.

*B*lack, Red, and White Currants

*B*lack currants are ideal fruits to grow on heavy, damp soil, and they will grow vigorously if the soil is rich in nutrients. Most black currant bushes are large, but there are some small, modern varieties available that are perfect for smaller gardens. Keep the plants well watered when the berries are swelling, and net the bushes to protect them from birds. When the fruits turn black, they are ripe. Prune the bushes in winter; cut back a few old stems (no more than one fifth of the total) to ground level, or to the junction with a strong, young shoot.

Both red and white currant bushes resemble small, upright black currant bushes. You can grow them as bushes or cordons, and care for them in the same way as gooseberries. Red currants have a sharp taste, and can be made into a tangy jelly to serve with lamb or poultry. They are also delicious mixed with strawberries and eaten raw. In mixed-berry tarts they balance the sweetness of the other fruits. White currants are always eaten raw, and taste similar to grapes. They look pretty sprinkled into fruit salads.

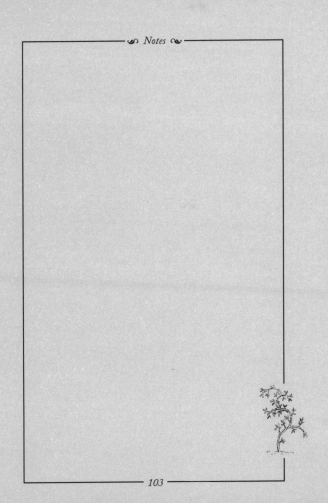

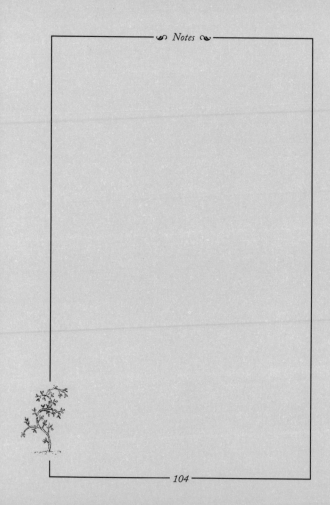

✍ *Notes* ✍

Cane Fruits

Cane fruits include blackberries, loganberries, and other hybrid berries with similar growth habits. Most bushes are extremely prickly and, by growing them on post-and-wire supports, you can have a very secure, productive garden boundary. A few thornless varieties are available but the flavor of the fruits can be inferior. Blackberries are not fussy about soil, and tolerate windy conditions well. All cane fruits are vigorous growers and need heavy feeding. Canes soon become unmanageable unless they are trained, and you should tie all the sprouts (shoots) out horizontally in the same direction. During the summer, strong new sprouts grow out from the bases of the plants. Tie these up loosely and keep them upright. After the fruits have been picked, cut off all the old canes close to the bases of the plants and tie the new canes to the wires.

Grapes

Grape vines make very decorative climbers on a wall or trellis or over an arch or pergola. Grown in this way, they need no special treatment, but will still produce a reasonable crop. Tie the new growth in place to keep the plants tidy, and shorten long shoots and thin out surplus stems in winter. If you want a large crop for either dessert fruit or wine-making, the vines are best grown on post-and-wire supports with the stems trained out horizontally.

Pruning can be complicated, so follow the illustrated directions you can find in specialist books. Vines need a very sunny spot and well-drained soil, amended with plenty of organic matter. Water during dry summers, as mildew can be troublesome if plants dry out. Don't use fungicides on grapes intended for wine-making, as they may affect fermentation. Feed the vines with high-potash tomato fertilizer every week in summer. Thin out dessert grapes so that the bunches contain fewer, but larger grapes. Use narrow-nosed grape scissors to remove about one third of the fruits when they are slightly less than pea-sized. The tiny grapes can be used in fruit tarts. In cold regions, dessert grapes should be grown in a greenhouse.

Passion Fruit

*P*assion fruits grow on large, climbing plants, which have spectacular flowers of red, purple, or blue. The best species to grow for fruiting are *Passiflora edulis*, *P. quadrangularis* (the giant granadilla), and *P. mollisima* (banana passion fruit). They need plenty of warmth, so grow them in a heated greenhouse or conservatory in cool regions. Grow a single plant in a large pot to restrict the roots, and train the stems up over a trellis on a sunny wall, spreading them out well. It may take a year or two before the plant starts fruiting. Hand-pollinate the flowers with a small artist's brush. Each

spring, prune the previous year's growth back to within 1in (2.5cm) of the main framework of branches.

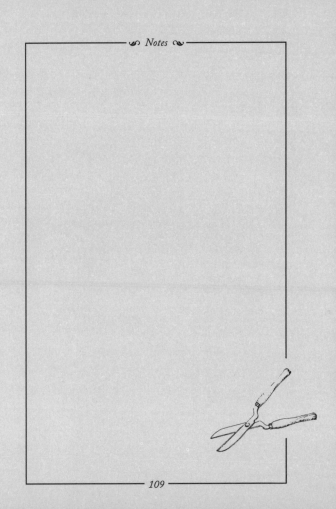

Kiwis

Kiwis, or Chinese gooseberries, are brown, oval, slightly hairy fruits that are green inside. The plants are large, attractive climbers that twine around trellises or poles for support. They will grow outside in all but the coldest regions, where they must be grown under glass and heavily pruned and trained if they are to produce a crop. Outdoors, in a warm, sunny spot, they will produce some fruits, but not maximum yields. Male and female flowers are produced on separate plants, which are sold under different names, and you will need a male and a female to produce fruits. Varieties of *Actinidia arguta*, which produce clusters of small fruits are self-fertile, so you need only one plant.

Citrus Fruits

Citrus fruits include grapefruits, lemons, oranges, and tangerines. There are also more unusual kinds, such as kumquats (small, oblong, orange-colored, bitter-tasting fruits used in cocktails and preserves), oddities such as the variegated lemons (which have green and gold patterned leaves and striped fruits), and hybrids, such as the limequat, which is a cross between a kumquat and a lime. Citrus trees are evergreen, decorative, and have strongly perfumed flowers, which often appear at the same time as the fruits. They need winter protection in cold regions, so grow them in pots and

move them into a heated greenhouse or conservatory where the temperature never drops below 50°F (10°C). In summer, set them out in a sunny, sheltered corner of the patio. The plants are happiest in lime-free soil, in containers just large enough to take their roots. Feed with liquid tomato fertilizer and water freely in summer. Keep them on the dry side in winter. To taste their full flavor, allow the fruits to ripen on the plants, by which time the rinds should be well-colored and the fruits should yield slightly when squeezed.

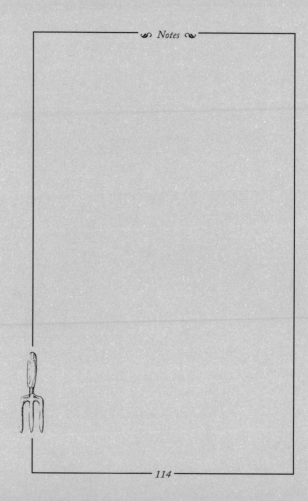

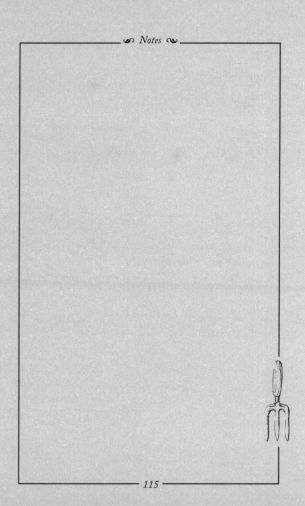

— ❧ *Notes* ❧ —

Trees from Seeds

When you bite into an exotic fruit from the supermarket, do you ever wonder what its parent plant looks like? To find out, you can plant the seeds. Tropical fruits, such as avocado pears, dates, litchis (lychees), mangoes, and rambutans, will not survive a cold winter outside, but they make fascinating indoor plants. They are unlikely to produce fruits indoors, but they do have good foliage. Sow the seeds straight from the fruits–if they dry out, they rarely grow. Sow in potting mix, water well, then seal the pot inside a plastic bag. Stand it in a warm place out of direct sunlight–a windowsill above a radiator is fine. When the seeds germinate, take the pots out of the bags. The plants will grow quickly–in their natural surroundings, most grow into huge trees. Treat them like any tropical houseplants.

Training Fruit Trees

*F*an-trained trees are ideal for growing against a wall, which is the perfect situation for warmth-loving kinds (such as peaches and nectarines, in cold regions), or for accommodating plums and cherries when there is no room in the garden for a standard tree. Routine care simply involves cutting out stems that grow outward, shortening the main branches when they grow too long, and tying in the new ones needed to continue the fan shape. ✒✒

✦✦

*C*ordon trees look more like broomsticks than trees, with fruit growing from clusters of short twigs. They can be grown 30in (75cm) apart, so you can fit several varieties into a small space. They are usually grown at an angle of 45°, which means that the top of a 9ft (2.5m) tree is only 5ft (1.5m) from the ground–a comfortable height for picking. A row of cordon trees make a good screen for dividing up a large garden or for hiding eyesores. Put up a 5ft- (1.5m-) high fence of posts and horizontal wires, then plant the trees. Tie the trunk of each to a strong stake and tie the stake to the support wires. Each year, in late summer, prune the sideshoots back to just above a cluster of developing fruits. Prune nonfruitful sideshoots to within 1in (2.5cm) of the current year's growth, which is soft and green. In winter, cut the top of the trunk back level with the top wire of your support fence.

ღ

*E*spaliers have tiers of horizontal branches growing out from a central trunk, and can be grown either against a wall or in the open with posts and wires supporting the branches. Each branch is pruned in the same way as a cordon tree. Fruits on espaliers ripen well, because they are not hidden by surrounding branches. Unless you fancy training fruit trees as a hobby and can wait several years for the shape to develop, buy young, ready trained trees from your nursery or garden center.

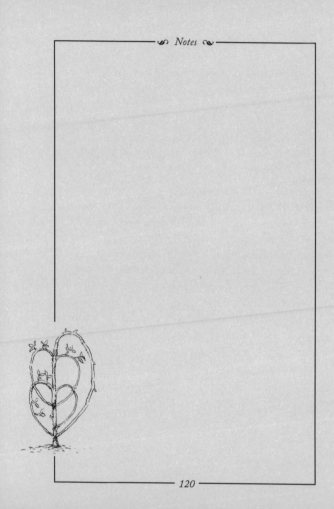

Pruning

Pruning is the thing that worries most people who grow fruit. It is not absolutely essential to prune, but if you don't the fruits will be small and poorly colored. Pruning thins out branches and lets light and air circulate around the plant, helping the fruits to ripen well and color properly. By reducing the number of branches, you reduce the amount of fruit the plant carries, so what is left receives more nutrients from the soil, and is bigger and of better quality. Unless you are an enthusiast, you need only thin out congested growth and cut out any dead, diseased, or damaged shoots.

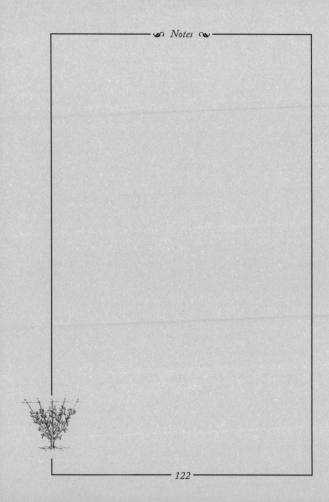

$\mathcal{A}$ good pair of pruning shears is the most important piece of equipment for anyone who grows fruit. I find it useful to have two pairs—one for rough pruning and tidying and a better-quality pair for precise work that needs a really sharp edge. There are two basic types of pruning shears—the more sophisticated (and more expensive), has two sharp blades that glide past each other with a scissor action. They give the best cut, and the blades can usually be removed for sharpening. The other type is known as anvil pruning shears. These have one blade that cuts down onto a rubber "stop" or flat plate. They are excellent when new, but once the blade becomes blunt it can cause bruising to the stems. Some anvil pruning shears have a ratchet action that makes cutting through tough stems easier, and is ideal if you have weak wrists or a touch of arthritis.

CHAPTER FOUR
Crop Rotation

∾

*Y*ou should avoid growing the same vegetables in the same bit of ground year after year. Each crop takes up different nutrients from the soil, and each carries its own soil diseases. The more often the crop is grown in the same spot, the more it depletes the soil of those nutrients, and the greater risk there is of soil-borne diseases building up.

∽∾

*R*otation allows the crops to be grown in a different spot each year. First, the vegetables are divided up into three or four groups, then the vegetable garden is divided into the same number of plots. In the first year, grow one group on each patch, then move everything around one place the following year. That way, the soil is correctly treated for each crop in turn and most problems are neatly avoided by good husbandry, rather than man-made remedies. Fruit and other permanent crops, such as asparagus, which cannot be moved every year, are not included in the rotation.

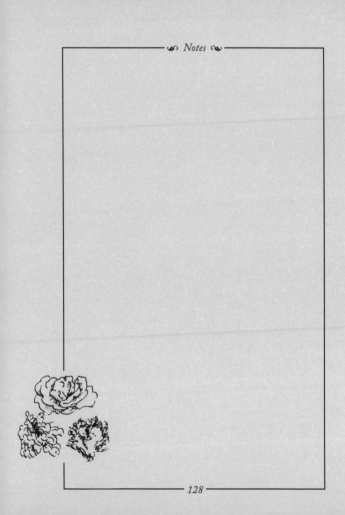

Plot one should be heavily manured in fall or winter; add a general fertilizer in spring and grow peas and beans, which like plenty of organic matter, in this plot. These plants have nodules on their roots that "fix" nitrogen from the air. After each crop, cut down the stems and leave the roots in the ground, where they will slowly release nitrogen into the soil to benefit the next crop.

Plot two should be lightly amended with well-rotted manure or compost in fall or winter. If the soil is acid or neutral, apply lime to raise the pH to a little over 7. Apply a general fertilizer shortly before planting and grow brassicas on this plot.

Plot three should not be manured, but should be given a generous application of general fertilizer shortly before planting. If the soil is poor when you first start the rotation, you can improve it by digging in some completely decomposed organic matter, such as thoroughly rotted garden compost, coir, old potting mix, or the used contents of growing bags, in the fall. This plot is for root crops, which fork or split if the soil contains too much nitrogen.

꙰

In a traditional rotation, the entire fourth plot would be used for potatoes, but if you want to grow only a few rows, plant them in plot three and use plot four for salad greens, spinach and other leafy crops, and sweet corn and outdoor tomatoes. Prepare the soil in the same way as plot one. Alternatively, take this plot out of the rotation and use it for perennial crops, such as asparagus and artichokes, or turn it into a herb garden.

Plot one   *Plot three*

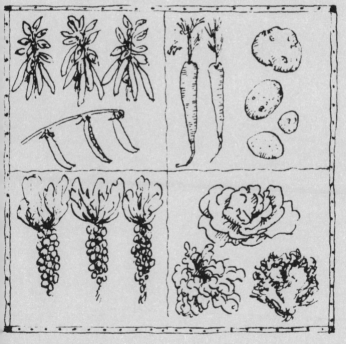

Plot two   *Plot four*

*I*f crop rotation is not practical, either because your garden is very small or because the crops you want to grow don't fit in with the traditional cropping plan, simply compromise. Plant what you want, but avoid growing the same crop in the same place two years running. In fall or winter, dig in organic matter everywhere except where you intend to grow root crops, but particularly where you will grow legumes (peas and beans). Always try to follow peas or beans with brassicas, so the brassicas can benefit from the extra nitrogen in the soil.

Catch-Crops

However well-planned your kitchen garden, gaps will begin to appear from midsummer onward, when crops, such as summer cabbages and overwintering onions, are finished. Instead of leaving the spaces empty, use them for fast-maturing crops that will be ready before the end of the season. Suitable crops to sow up to midsummer include bush beans, lettuces, spinach, salad greens, and early varieties of peas and carrots, which are faster growing than maincrop varieties. In early fall, plant spring cabbages or onion sets for overwintering.

Intercropping

Intercropping makes the most of every bit of space in a small kitchen garden. Sow or plant fast-maturing crops, particularly spinach, lettuces, and bush beans, between rows of slower-growing plants, such as sweet corn, maincrop potatoes, and Brussels sprouts—the intercropped plants will be harvested by the time the foliage of the main crops covers the rows. This technique is only suitable for traditional kitchen gardens, where plants are grown at conventional wide spacings. On deep beds, the intercropped plants would be smothered by the foliage of the main crops.

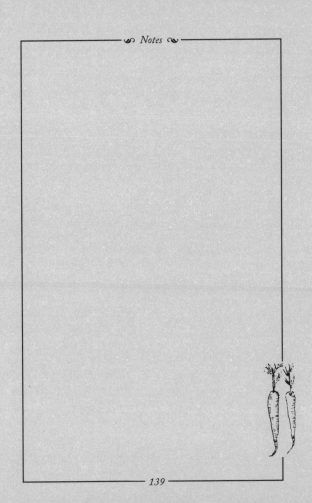

CHAPTER FIVE
Food for the Soil

❧

$\mathcal{M}$y grandfather had a good way of recycling his kitchen garden refuse. He kept hens on his plot and threw all the cabbage stalks, lettuce leaves, and similar debris into their pen, where they converted it into manure much more quickly than the compost heap ever could. Every fall, when most of the crops had been cleared, he'd let the hens out. While they were enjoying themselves, scratching around and feeding on the weeds, insect pests, and crop debris, grandad and I would take the strawy manure from their run and put it on the compost heap.

Compost

Use healthy, green materials, such as lawn mowings, the outer leaves of vegetables, annual weeds, and kitchen scraps to make a compost heap. Don't use diseased plants and perennial weeds as you may spread spores or roots around the garden. Woody materials, such as tree prunings, take a long time to rot down, and need to be cut up finely, or put through a garden shredder before they are added to the heap.

*I*f you want good compost quickly, don't just pile the materials up in a heap–buy, or make compost bins. In an enclosed space compost materials heat up fast, and in warm conditions the compost should be ready to use within three months. Construct containers from planks, and make them 3ft (1m) square and the same height. Leave 1in (2.5cm) gaps between the planks to allow air to get in, and make covers for the tops.

❧❧

*F*ill the first bin with alternating 6in- (15cm) deep layers of lawn clippings, weeds, crop debris, and household waste. A mixture of materials is vital if you want well-textured compost that is neither slimy, nor too dry. Firm each layer down, damp it if necessary, and top it with a 1in (2.5cm) layer of garden soil or animal manure to hold in the moisture and provide the natural bacteria and nitrogen needed to activate the heap. Continue building up the layers until the bin is full, then cover the top–a piece of old carpet makes good cover. Depending on the time of year, the compost will take between 3 and 12 months before it is ready.

Worm Compost

A worm bin looks like a garbage can with a tap near the bottom, and its job is to make worm compost, an organic, soillike substance, which is rich in nutrients and trace elements. To set up a wormery, put a layer of drainage material in the bottom of the container, cover it with some well-rotted compost, then add the worms (take some from your compost heap or buy them in a fishing-tackle shop). Every day, add a layer of chopped, fresh, green material, such as kitchen waste, vegetable leaves, or weeds. The worms will digest the waste and replace it with worm castings. When the container is full of compost, empty it, salvage the worms, and start again. Use the tap to drain off the liquid that is produced during the process, dilute it with water, and use it as a liquid fertilizer. Spread the worm compost around your vegetables.

Manure

Animal manures vary enormously in quality. Manure from intensive farms may contain chemical residues from foodstuff additives, and is best avoided. If possible, use manure from riding stables and organic farms and stack it for a year, until it looks like fibrous compost, before you use it. Small amounts of fresh manure can be added to the compost heap as an accelerator.

Green Manure

Green manures are grown specially to dig into the soil to improve its texture. Suitable plants include agricultural lupins, alfalfa, mustard, and phacelia. These should be sown thickly any time during the growing season, then dug in before they flower. Sow grazing rye, tares, and field beans, which are particularly beneficial for clay soil, in late summer and leave them to stand through the winter, then dig them in six weeks before you want to plant or sow the plot. Green manure crops are easier to dig in if you cut them down and leave them to dry out first.

Seaweed

Seaweed is a useful bonus for gardeners who live near the coast, but always obtain permission before gathering it. Avoid seaweed contaminated by oil, tar, or similar flotsam, and wash the fronds to remove salt or lay them out on a gravel path for a few weeks in the rain. Fresh seaweed can be dug in to the soil in the fall, and will have decomposed by planting time. Alternatively, you can add it in layers to the compost heap. Seaweed is a good source of potash and trace elements, and inland gardeners can buy dried seaweed meal and liquid seaweed extract from organic garden suppliers.

Leaf Mold

*I*nstead of burning fallen leaves in autumn, convert them into valuable leaf mold. Pile them into a "cage," made by tacking wire netting around four posts driven into the ground to make a square container. Dampen each load of leaves as you add them and firm them down well. When the cage is full, cover the top with 1in (2.5cm) of soil. After about two years, the leaf mold should look fine and crumbly. Use it to mulch woodland plants and as a substitute for peat.

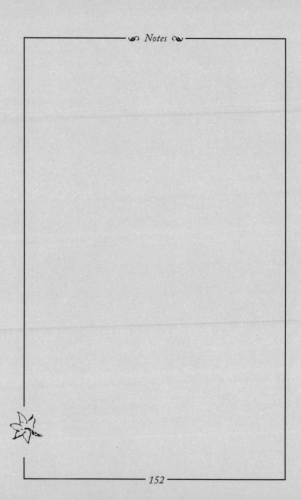

ও *Notes* ও

Organic Granular Fertilizers

*M*any organic fertilizers and liquid feeds are available. If your local garden center doesn't stock them, look in gardening magazines or directories to find the addresses of mail-order organic garden suppliers. Organic sources of nitrogen include hoof and horn meal and blood meal. For phosphate, use bonemeal (that is very slow-acting) or rock phosphate. Organic sources of potash can sometimes be bought, but you can use wood ash from bonfires or wood-burning stoves. Fish, blood, and bone meal is a good general fertilizer, but it contains sulfate of potash, which is not truly organic. Liquid feeds made from fish or manure are available, and seaweed extract, worm compost, good-quality garden compost, and manure all provide valuable trace elements.

Organic Liquid Fertilizers

*Y*ou can brew your own liquid plant food, made from comfrey. Special varieties of comfrey are sold by organic garden suppliers, but Russian comfrey *(Symphytum officinale)* is nearly as good. The roots of comfrey penetrate very deeply into the soil and draw up minerals that are then stored in the leaves, that can be cut several times a year. Stand a water barrel (one that has a tap near the bottom) on some bricks to raise it high enough for you to fill a watering can from it. Fill the barrel with comfrey leaves, then top it off with water. Leave to brew for a month or so, then draw off the liquid, dilute it with an equal quantity of water, and use it to feed tomatoes and fruit. Use a weaker solution to feed other vegetables, and young, or less robust plants. When the barrel is empty, throw the comfrey on the compost heap and start again.

Always use liquid feeds, or soluble fertilizers diluted at the correct rate, to feed containerized plants—solid fertilizer is too concentrated and may scorch the roots. Liquid feeds are good for plants in greenhouse borders too. In the garden, use them when the ground is dry and solid fertilizers would not be dissolved, or whenever plants need a quick boost. Liquid fertilizers allow you to apply the appropriate nutrient when the plants need it. High-potash tomato fertilizers are good for all flowering plants, but dilute them to half or quarter the rate used for tomatoes. High-nitrogen fertilizers are best for foliage plants, and to give a quick boost to anything that is not growing well. (These fertilizers can also be used, very much diluted, for foliar feeding, which allows the plants to take up nutrients even more quickly.) Organic liquid seaweed extract can be added to foliar feeds, to supply trace elements.

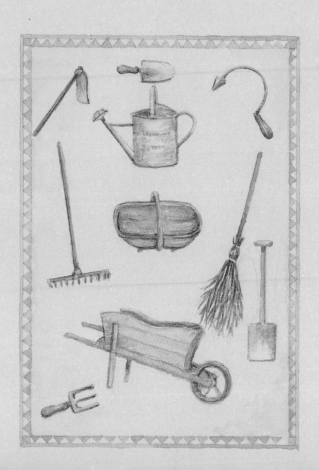

CHAPTER SIX

Doing the Groundwork

❧

Tools

Kitchen gardening doesn't need a lot of special equipment. In addition to the basic tools—a spade and fork for digging, a hoe for weeding, a rake for preparing the soil, and a trowel for planting—you will need a pair of good pruning shears and a garden line to help get the rows straight when you are sowing or planting—you can make your own from two short stakes and a ball of string or a wooden board marked into convenient planting distances such as 6in (15cm) and 1ft (30cm). Other useful items include stakes, bean poles, and netting.

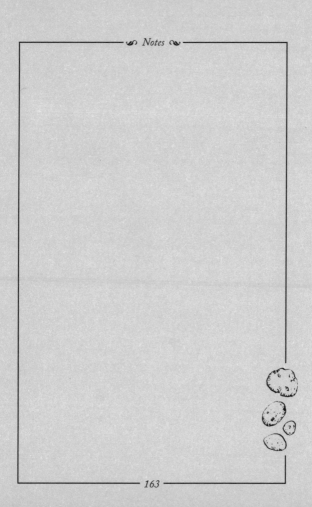

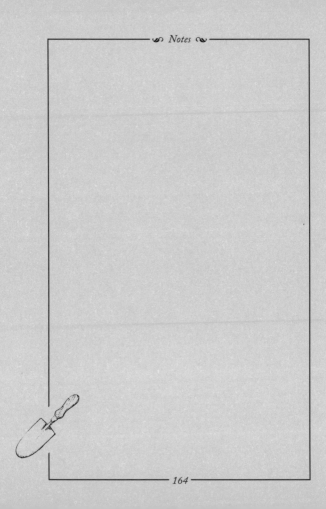

Testing the Soil

One of the first things you should do when starting a kitchen garden is have the soil tested. A professional analysis can tell you how acid or alkaline your soil is (its pH value) and which nutrients it lacks, as well as what is needed to replenish them. Alternatively, you can buy a small soil-testing kit from the garden center. If you think the soil pH may vary around the garden, make separate tests. Most vegetables do best around pH 7, which is neutral—neither acid nor alkaline. Brassicas, peas, and fruits, such as cherries and plums, prefer a slightly higher pH (alkaline soil), while raspberries and blueberries need a lower pH (acid soil).

Dealing with Perennial Weeds

Before you plant the kitchen garden, you will need to get rid of perennial weeds. If you don't want to resort to chemical solutions, you can either sow grass and keep the area mowed until no more perennial weeds come up or cover the soil with black plastic, old carpet, or something similar, that will exclude the light.

Spading

Spading is the first step in preparing the soil. When making new beds, it is worth double digging. Dig a trench one spade deep and move the displaced soil to the other end of the plot. Fork organic matter into the base of the trench, then dig the next trench alongside it, using the soil to fill the first one. Continue in this way across the plot, using the soil from the first trench to fill the last one. In future, it will be sufficient to spread organic matter over the surface of the plot, and turn it in with a fork or spade.

Preparing Deep Beds

*D*eep beds are very productive, and require very little work once they have been constructed, but they do take quite a bit of effort to make in the first place. First, mark out the area. The beds should be narrow enough to let you reach the middle from each side. Don't make them too long either, as you'll get tired of walking around them. Double-dig the beds, adding as much well-rotted organic matter as possible, then never walk on them again, so the soil does not become compacted. Lay paved or gravel paths between the beds for easy access. On waterlogged or clay soils, where deep cultivation is not practical, edge the beds with planks and built up the soil to make raised beds instead.

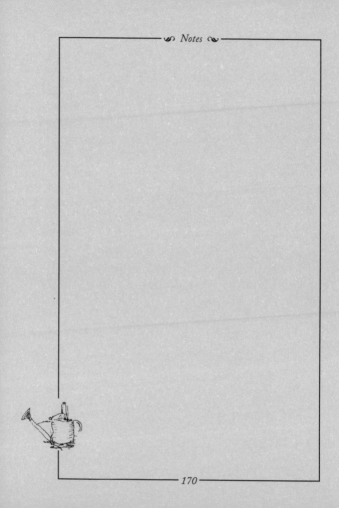

Improving Clay Soil

In wet weather, clay soil turns to mud and in drought it sets hard and may even crack. The best way to improve clay is to dig in at least one bucketful of sand per square yard (square metre). You will need to do this only once. The sand opens up the structure of the soil, aerating it and improving surface drainage. Every year, dig in as much organic matter as possible. If the soil is too wet in winter, do it in spring to avoid compacting the clay when it is wet.

Paths

Good paths make all the difference in a kitchen garden, and form part of the structure of ornamental gardens such as potagers. Bare soil may look "natural" but it soon turns to mud in wet weather, and quickly grows a covering of weeds, and grass paths need mowing and may start balding if used over-much. The best paths have hard surfaces, such as gravel or paving, laid over a foundation of hardcore. Gravel paths need to be edged with tiles, bricks, or planks of wood to stop the gravel from spreading sideways into the beds.

Seeds

Most of the vegetable seeds sold today are of F1 hybrids. This means the variety has been produced by crossing two specific parents; the same cross has to be made again to get more seeds of the same variety. This explains why F1 seeds are so expensive and why it is no good saving seed from F1 hybrid plants–their progeny do not breed true. Since few new vegetable varieties are bred with the home-grower in mind, it is common to find "commercial" characteristics, such as high yields and pest and disease resistance, as features of F1 varieties. (The latter makes them ideal for organic growing, because the need to use insecticides and pesticides is reduced.) Modern varieties are also bred to crop all at once for easy harvesting; at home, this is fine if you grow for freezing, but if you prefer to eat your vegetables fresh it's nice to be able to pick a little and often.

The alternative to F1 hybrids is "open-pollinated" varieties. These are older varieties that breed true from seed—heritage vegetables fall into this category—so you can save your own seed, which is not only a good way to cut down the cost of vegetable growing, butalso enables you to grow rare varieties that are not easy to buy. Although the plants breed true from seed, insects may cross-pollinate them with other crops of the same type so, unless you are the only person in your area growing winter squashes, for example, you should hand-pollinate them to be sure of getting the true variety. Using a small artist's brush, transfer pollen from a male flower to a female flowerof the same variety, then tie a cheesecloth or paper bag over a female flower. Wait until the petals fade before removing the bag, then label the developing fruit so you can distinguish it from the others when you come to collect the seeds.

Preparing the Seed Bed

*I*f you sow vegetable seeds into rough, lumpy, or stony soil, many of them will not germinate. Choose a sheltered spot where the soil has been well cultivated previously, and make a seed bed. Spade up (dig over) the bed, removing weeds as you go, but don't add any organic matter unless it is so thoroughly rotted it resembles soil. Rake the surface well to remove stones, roots, or other debris, then sprinkle with a general fertilizer and rake it in. Continue raking until the soil resembles cake crumbs. You now have a fine tilth, which is ready to be sown.

Annual Weed Seeds

*I*t can be very frustrating to sow seeds, only to see masses of weeds come up and swamp the seedlings. To prevent this, you must rid the soil of annual weed seeds. Instead of preparing your seedbed just before sowing, do it several months in advance, but don't add any fertilizer. Once a week, lightly hoe the surface of the soil. This will not bring fresh weed seeds to the surface, but it will disturb germinating seeds and kill them. By doing this regularly, all the seeds in the top layer of soil will be uncovered and encouraged to germinate before you sow your vegetables.

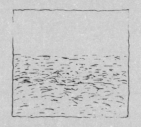

Sowing Outdoors

When your seedbed is ready, use a garden line to mark out a straight row, then draw the back of a hoe blade along the edge of the line to make a drill about ½in (1.5cm) deep for small seeds or 1in (2.5cm) deep for larger ones. Sprinkle small seeds very thinly along the drill and space larger ones individually, then rake the soil very gently to just cover them. In heavy clay soil, where seeds often rot, or light, sandy soil, where seedlings can dry out quickly, you can improve the germination rate by sprinkling ¼in (0.5cm) of vermiculite along the drills before you sow and using more of the same to cover the seeds. Keep seeds and the seedlings well watered.

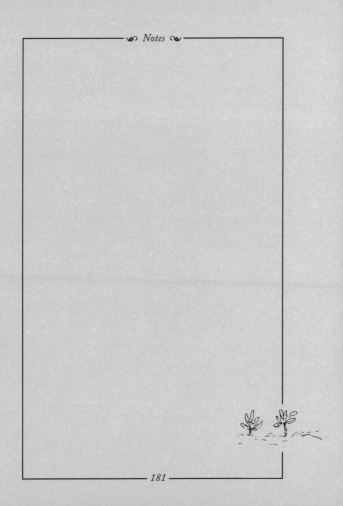

Thinning and Transplanting

Vegetable seedlings come up quite thickly when sown in rows. You won't need all the plants, so wait until they are large enough to handle, then thin them out, leaving the strongest about 1in (2.5cm) apart. By the time the plants are 2-4in (5-10cm) tall, depending on what you are growing, they will be ready to transplant into their final positions in the garden. Prepare the planting site, then use a hand fork to dig up each seedling, taking care not to damage its roots. Dig a hole with the trowel, and, holding the seedling by a leaf, lower it in place and spread out the roots. Adjust the height so the lower leaves are just above soil level, then fill around the roots with soil and water well.

Hoeing Out Invaders

Weeds are constant, if unwelcome, occupants of the kitchen garden. Their seeds are always present in the soil and germinate whenever they are brought to the surface by cultivation. By preventing weeds from seeding you can gradually reduce the population in the soil, but this takes time. In the meantime, it is vital to stop weeds from smothering the crops. The best method of control is regular hoeing. Many different types of hoes are available—try several and choose the one that suits you best. Hoe often, before the weeds grow tall. If they get out of hand among the vegetables, use a small hand fork or hand weed carefully around the plants. Once the vegetables grow up and cast shade over the soil between the rows, weeding will be less of a problem. Deep beds need less work because the plants are grown close together and the foliage smothers the weeds more quickly.

Sowing Under Glass

In cooler areas, if you want to grow frost-tender plants or if you want early crops of hardy ones, you can raise the seedlings in a greenhouse, or on a warm, sunny windowsill indoors. Loosely fill clean flats with potting mix and firm it lightly. Water well, then scatter the seeds very thinly on top. Sieve a little more potting mix over the top, to barely cover them. Place the flats in a well-lit place out of direct sunlight until the seeds germinate, taking care not to let the growing medium dry out.

Sowing in Pots

Large seeds are easy to handle and germinate quickly. You can cut out a lot of work by sowing them individually in small pots. Fill the pots with potting mix and push one seed into each pot until it is buried to roughly its own depth. Water well and set in a warm place, out of direct sunlight. When the seedlings are 3-4in (7.5-10cm) high, and the pots are filled with roots, harden them off and plant them out.

If you are sewing small seeds, try a method called multi-seeding. Sow several seeds in each pot of potting mix and raise them under cover. This method is suitable for growing plants that have small seeds such as onions, leeks, cabbages, salad leaves, and herbs. When the seedlings come up, weed out the weakest to leave three or four to grow on. When the pots are full of roots, harden off the plants, then plant them out, still in their clumps, but at 2-3 times the usual spacings—they will reach normal size, and produce normal crops.

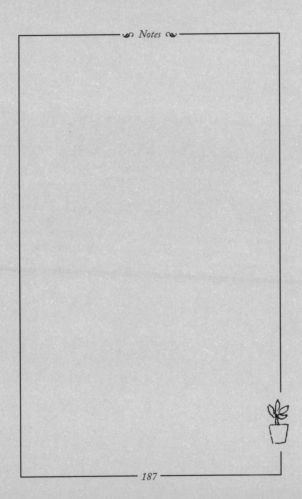

Pricking Out

*W*hen seedlings first come up, they each have a pair of baby "seed leaves." By the time they have one or two true leaves as well, they need more space. Prepare a new flat and make a hole in the potting mix for each seedling. Use a dibber or the tip of a pencil to loosen the seedlings. Remove them one at a time, taking care not to damage the roots. Lift each seedling by holding a leaf, to avoid bruising the stem, and replant carefully in the new flat, spacing 1-2in (1.5-2.5cm) apart. Plant the seedlings with their bottom leaves just above soil level. Set the flats in a well-lit place, and give just enough water to keep the potting mix evenly moist. When the plants are large enough, harden them off, then plant them out.

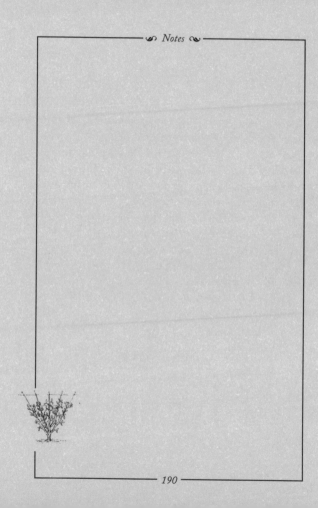

Hardening Off

Plants that have been started off indoors must be hardened off for two or three weeks before they are planted out, to accustom them gradually to the colder, windier conditions outdoors. Harden them off in a cold frame, if you have one. Move the plants to the frame and keep the lid down at first, then raise it on fine days, and slowly increase the plants' exposure to the open air, until the lid is only closed at night. Finally, leave the lid up at night too, except when cold weather is forecast. If you don't have a cold frame, set the plants outside in the garden on fine days, bringing them back in at night until it the weather is warm enough to plant them out safely in the garden.

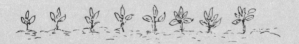

Planting Out

While the plants are hardening off, prepare the soil where they will be planted. Rake in the fertilizer and leave the surface level. (Firm the soil in the brassica bed by treading it with your heels before the final raking.) To plant the seedlings, use a trowel to dig a hole a little bigger than the pot, then upend the pot, and tap the base sharply with the trowel. Keep the rootball intact, and place the seedling in the hole so the top of the rootball is very slightly lower than the surrounding soil. Fill around the rootball with soil and firm gently in place, leaving a shallow depression around the plant to aid watering. Keep the plants well watered until they are established.

Notes

Succession Crops

During the growing season, there will be several changes of plants in the kitchen garden. As soon as you have harvested early crops of lettuces, spring cabbages, and potatoes, clear the ground, and put in the next crop as quickly as possible. There is no need to spade the soil again, but sprinkle some general fertilizer along the rows to replace nutrients, and fork over lightly. Rake well, then plant or sow.

Crop Protection

*F*loating row covers (horticultural fleece) are the modern equivalent of cloches, and help to extend the growing season by allowing plants to be set out earlier in spring, and by keeping late crops safe from frosts in fall. In spring, prepare the soil and cover it with black plastic to warm it up. Remove the plastic and sow or plant as usual, then drape the floating row cover over the bed and bury the edges in the soil, or use stones or bricks to hold it down. Leave it over the plants until the weather warms up and the plants are growing well, but remove it in hot weather or they may overheat. Toward the end of the season, when cold weather threatens, spread the covers over late crops, such as lettuces, baby carrots, and late peas, to keep them growing for as long as possible. Use them to protect late crops of frost-tender vegetables, such as bush beans and zucchini.

Synthetic Mulches

*I*f you want a totally weed-free kitchen garden without doing any weeding, use a permanent mulch of black plastic. This may not look too good, but it certainly looks better than an overgrown patch of weeds. Use special slitted or perforated black plastic sold for the purpose. Unroll it over the ground after preparing the soil, stretch it out flat, and hold it in place with wire pegs or stones. Cut X-shapes in the plastic, peel back the flaps, plant through the holes, then tuck the flaps around the plants so that no soil is exposed to light. Water, liquid feeds, and air can reach the soil through the tiny holes or slits, but few weeds will germinate because the plastic excludes most of the light. Use a heavy-duty plastic for fruit trees, bushes, and other permanent crops and a lightweight type, which can be thrown away at the end of the season, for vegetables.

Planting Trees

Container-grown fruit trees and bushes can be planted at any time of year except when the ground is frozen, very muddy, or very dry, but fall and spring are the best times to plant them, if you can. Dig a hole several times larger than the size of the pot, and mix plenty of well-rotted compost or manure in the bottom, then hammer in a stake to support the tree. If planting in spring, mix in some general fertilizer—in fall, use bonemeal. Remove the plant from its pot and place it in the hole. Check the level—the top of the rootball should be flush with the surrounding soil. Adjust the level if necessary, then fill in round the roots with a mixture of soil, and compost or manure. Water the tree well and secure it to the stake with a tree tie, which will not chafe the bark in windy weather. Bareroot trees must be planted right away, or the roots will dry out. Plant in the same way as container-grown plants, but spread the roots out in the bottom of the hole. To find the correct planting depth, look for the ring of soil on the trunk and plant to that level.

Notes

Watering

Most vegetables need a great deal of water, so it's a good idea to equip the kitchen garden with a tap, especially if it is some distance from the house, and keep a hose and watering can handy. Newly planted vegetables need the most water, but in a dry summer all crops need watering, or they will become tough and stringy or run to seed. Fruit trees, canes, and bushes need watering until they become established, but after that they can, for the most part, take care of themselves. In dry summers, it is worth watering soft fruits, particularly strawberries, while the fruits are swelling. When you water, do so very thoroughly, then wait until the plants need watering again—don't water little and often. Direct the water to the bases of the plants and let it soak in—don't sprinkle it over the surface—it will just evaporate. In hot weather, water in the evening so the plants have all night to take up the water before it evaporates.

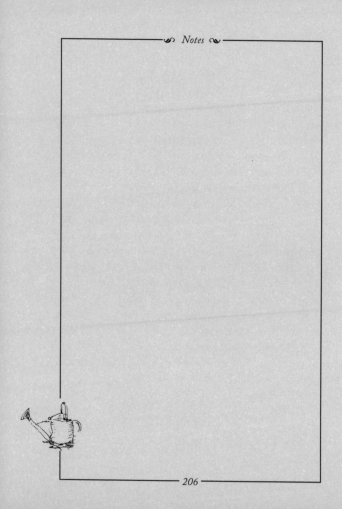

Notes

Pests and Diseases

$\mathcal{N}$owadays, few kitchen gardeners are keen to use chemical pesticides, both out of consideration for wildlife and the environment and because they will be eating the produce themselves. As soon as you stop using pesticides, beneficial insects will begin to colonize the garden and keep pest levels down. If you provide facilities to encourage beneficials, you will soon have a thriving population. They need places to overwinter, nectar for adults to feed on, and undisturbed areas in which to breed—a border of wildflowers around the garden will provide everything they need. For a more decorative effect, surround the garden with old-fashioned hardy annuals or plant an herb garden, and leave dead stems untouched throughout the winter.

*T*here is nothing worse than spending months caring for a crop, only to find that a sudden plague of pests seems determined to ruin it. When this happens, many gardeners turn to organic sprays, because natural predators would be unable to remove the attackers in time. There is no need to spray the whole kitchen garden—treat only the plants that are affected, and be sure to choose an organic measure such as rotenone-pyrethrum, insecticidal soap, or BT (*Bacillus thurginiensis*). Always follow the makers' instructions precisely, spray in the evening to avoid harming bees, and don't spray in windy weather, or onto open flowers. Do not eat, freeze, or preserve sprayed crops until after the interval indicated on the product label, which may vary from one day to two weeks, depending on the product.

*Y*ou can protect plants from harmful pests with fine-mesh netting, which is sold by mail-order organic garden suppliers and some garden centers. Use the netting to cover seedbeds or young plants. Tuck it around and under the plants–tie it around the bases of brassica stems–and leave it in place throughout the life of the crop. Check that the plants are not harboring pests before you cover them, or the pests will breed inside the mesh. In the greenhouse, use biological controls to protect plants, or stand pots outside for a few weeks to clear outbreaks without spraying.

If growing conditions are good, vegetables rarely suffer from problems. "Good growing conditions" means that the soil and situation are right, and the plants are regularly fed and watered to keep them growing steadily, without setbacks. When plants are placed under stress, pests and diseases can become serious problems. There is generally no need to spray if they are caught in time. Small infestations of aphids, caterpillars, or other pests can be removed by hand.

CHAPTER SEVEN
Reaping the Benefits

Dealing with Gluts

*H*owever well you plan the kitchen garden, sooner or later you will get a glut of something. Usually, you will be able to freeze the surplus, but some vegetables (lettuces and cucumbers for example) don't freeze successfully. To avoid wasting them, cook them in dishes that make good use of large amounts of produce. Surplus lettuces can be cooked with green peas or used like spinach, and you can grate cucumbers into plain yogurt to make tzatziki to accompany kebabs or to use as a dip with Indian food.

❧❧

*F*reezing is the most reliable way of storing surplus crops. It is a good way to prevent gluts of fruit from becoming overripe, when you do not have time to make jam or wine immediately. If you are in a hurry, you can freeze prepared fruits and vegetables without blanching, but the storage time will be reduced. My favorite way of using excess tomatoes, peppers, and eggplants is to make ratatouille, which freezes much more successfully than the ingredients do if frozen separately.

Fruit

Soft fruits don't ripen all at once—you can pick over the same bushes, canes, or strawberry plants for several weeks and find ripe fruits almost daily. Most soft fruits are best eaten right away or cooked the same day. Refrigerate them immediately after picking and freeze surplus crops. Eat plums and cherries straight from the tree, or use them for cooking or making jams. Any surplus can be frozen and used for cooking later. Early-ripening varieties of apples and pears should not be stored. Eat early apples straight from the tree, and pick pears and bring them into a warm room for a few days, until they are soft and ready to eat. Pick late-ripening apples and pears in fall, before gales blow them down. Select only perfect ones to store, to avoid rotting. They will keep for a few weeks in the salad compartment of the fridge, or you can pack them in plastic bags that have a few air holes, and store them in a cool shed or garage for 6-8 weeks. For longer storage, lay the fruits out, not quite touching, on slatted shelves in a shed or store-room with a constant temperature of 45-50°F (7-10°C) and average humidity.

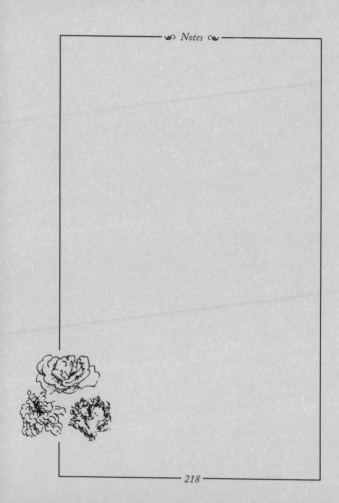

Herbs

Herbs can be preserved by chopping and freezing in ice cube containers with a teaspoonful of water, but drying is more convenient for large quantities. Gather herbs before they start flowering, and wash them only if absolutely necessary. If you have the space, spread them out on drying racks. Otherwise, hang them upside down in a warm, shady, well-ventilated place. You can peg small bunches to a drying rack on the kitchen ceiling for decoration, but never dry herbs for culinary use in a room where temperatures fluctuate or where vapor gathers. When the leaves are completely dry but still green, remove them carefully from the stems and store in dark-colored glass jars.

Vegetables

Vegetables are best used straight from the garden, but sometimes, if you have too much of some, or you want to save them to use in winter, you will need to store them. Where possible, leave maincrop roots, such as potatoes and carrots, in the ground, and dig them up as you need them. Once frosts threaten, dig them up, spread them out to dry without washing them (they keep longer if left dirty), then store them in paper bags in a frost-free shed or garage or in a root cellar. Winter-hardy crops, such as Savoy cabbages, Brussels sprouts, and leeks, are best left in the ground and harvested when you need them. Surplus summer roots and brassicas are best frozen. Blanch and skin tomatoes, or make them into a purée before freezing. Cut peppers and eggplants into chunks, or make them into prepared dishes. Salad crops, such as lettuces, can't be frozen, but oriental vegetables and spinach can.

The Last of the Harvest

$\mathcal{A}$t the end of the growing season, there may be some part-grown, or unripe crops left behind, but they can often be put to good use. Small beans, peppers, and eggplants, for example, can be cooked as usual, and half-grown cucumbers can be grated or cubed. Pick unripe tomatoes as soon as frost is forecast. Full-sized green tomatoes will ripened if you put them into a plastic bag with a ripe banana, and keep them out of sunlight at around 60°F (15°C)—the banana gives off ethylene gas, which does the trick. Don't leave tomatoes to ripen on a sunny windowsill, they'll wrinkle instead of ripening. Small, green tomatoes will never ripen, but you can use them to make chutney.

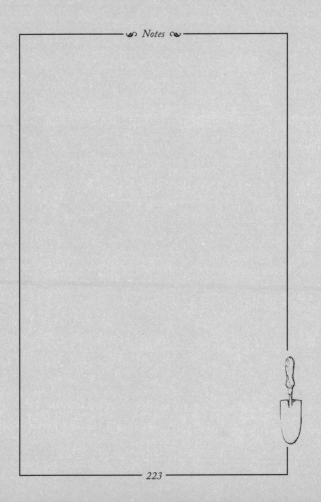

ⅎ *Notes* ⅎ

A FRIEDMAN/FAIRFAX BOOK

Library of Congress Cataloging-in-Publication Data available upon
request.

ISBN: 1-56799-611-6

Edited and produced by MQ Publications Ltd.
Text © Sue Phillips 1998
Illustrations © Anny Evason 1998
Editor: Linda Tsiricos
Designer: Bet Ayer

Printed in Hong Kong

1 3 5 7 9 10 8 6 4 2

For bulk purchases and special sales, please contact:
Friedman/Fairfax Publishers
Attention: Sales Department
15 West 26th Street
New York, New York 10010
212/685-6610   FAX 212/685-1307

Visit our website:
http://www.metrobooks.com